Very Important Adult Work, Totally Not a Coloring Book

Floral

Copyright © 2015 Savetz Publishing, Inc.

www.SavetzPublishing.com

All rights reserved. No part of this book may be reproduced in any form without written permission from the author.

ISBN 978-1-939169-03-7

Printed in the United States of America

Relax with Florals

The adult world has too many limitations on time, energy, and fun. The moment you apply pen—or crayon—or paint—to these coloring pages, though, you'll find those limitations slipping away. Creativity has a way of removing borders and opening up a world of relaxation and meditation.

The floral-themed coloring pages in this book will speak to you in different ways because of their range in pattern and style. You might find yourself drawn to a straightforward depiction of a gothic rose. You might lose yourself in the intricate design created by interwoven vines. Regardless of the picture, you'll find yourself in a better frame of mind and with an energized sense of creativity and imagination.

Use colored pencils, pens, or crayons to create unique effects and to draw out bold patterns. Unleash the secrets of each picture in whatever way suits your fancy. Color inside or outside the lines, frame your results, or choose another picture to unlock.

Also available for your coloring pleasure:

Mandala Coloring Pages, ISBN 978-1-939169-04-4
Geometric Coloring Pages, ISBN 978-1-939169-05-1

Visit

www.AdultColoringPages.net

for more coloring goodness

Visit
www.AdultColoringPages.net
for more coloring goodness

Visit

www.AdultColoringPages.net

for more coloring goodness

Visit
www.AdultColoringPages.net
for more coloring goodness

Visit

www.AdultColoringPages.net

for more coloring goodness

Visit

www.AdultColoringPages.net

for more coloring goodness

Visit
www.AdultColoringPages.net
for more coloring goodness

Visit
www.AdultColoringPages.net
for more coloring goodness

Visit
www.AdultColoringPages.net
for more coloring goodness

Visit

www.AdultColoringPages.net

for more coloring goodness

Visit
www.AdultColoringPages.net
for more coloring goodness

Visit
www.AdultColoringPages.net
for more coloring goodness

Visit
www.AdultColoringPages.net
for more coloring goodness

Visit

www.AdultColoringPages.net

for more coloring goodness

Visit

www.AdultColoringPages.net

for more coloring goodness

Visit
www.AdultColoringPages.net
for more coloring goodness

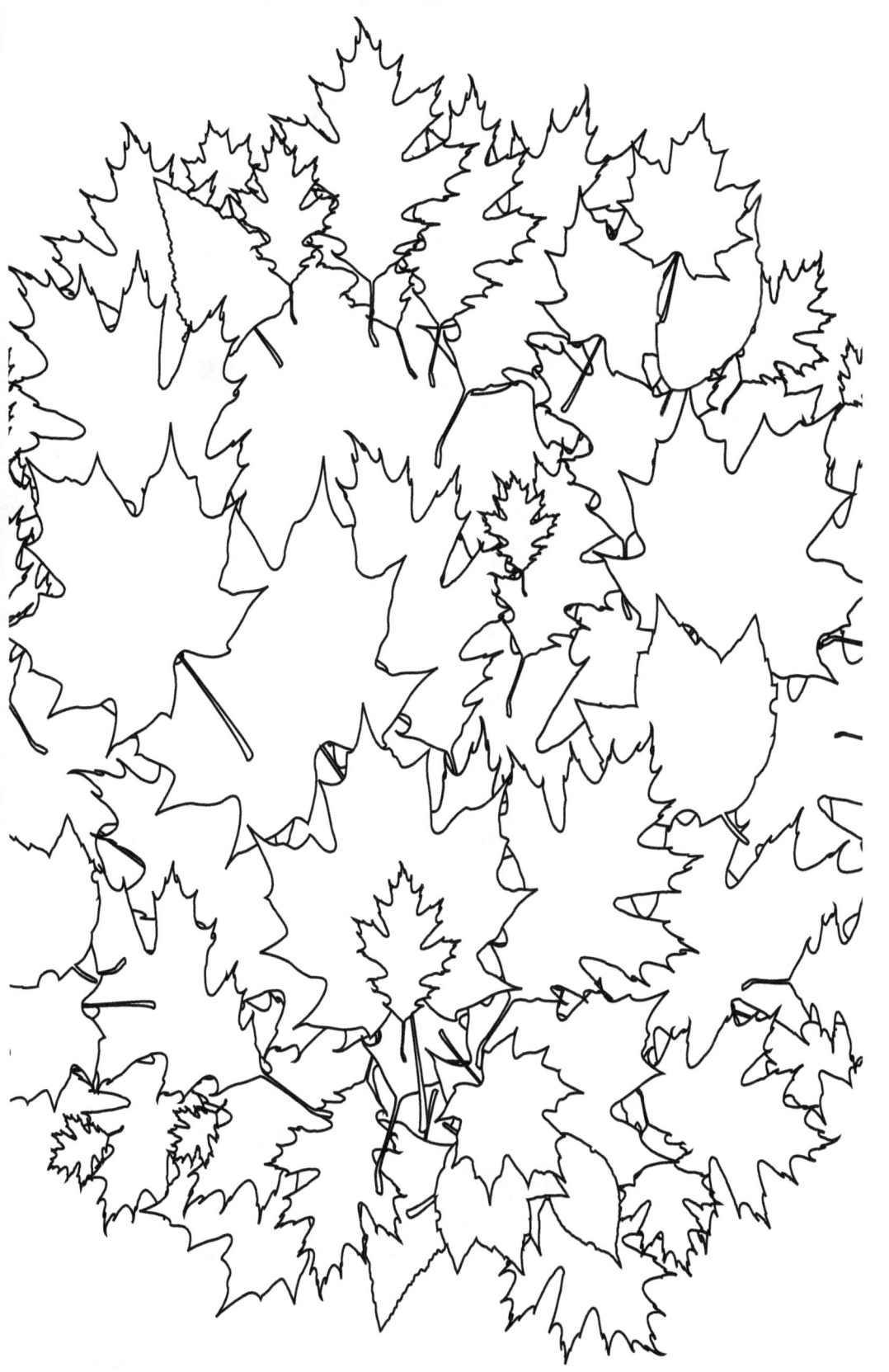

Visit

www.AdultColoringPages.net

for more coloring goodness

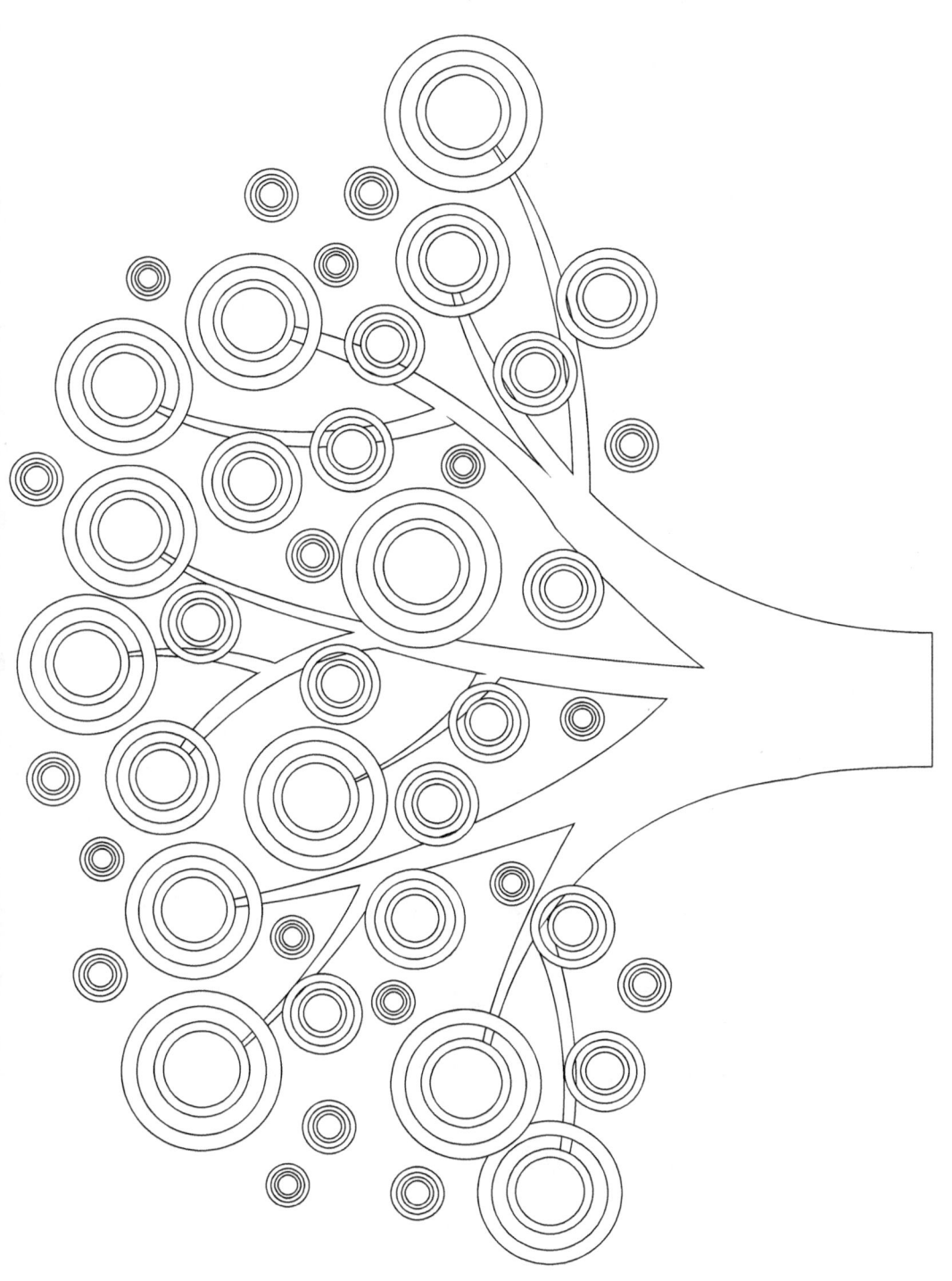

Visit

www.AdultColoringPages.net

for more coloring goodness

Visit
www.AdultColoringPages.net
for more coloring goodness

Visit

www.AdultColoringPages.net

for more coloring goodness

Visit
www.AdultColoringPages.net
for more coloring goodness

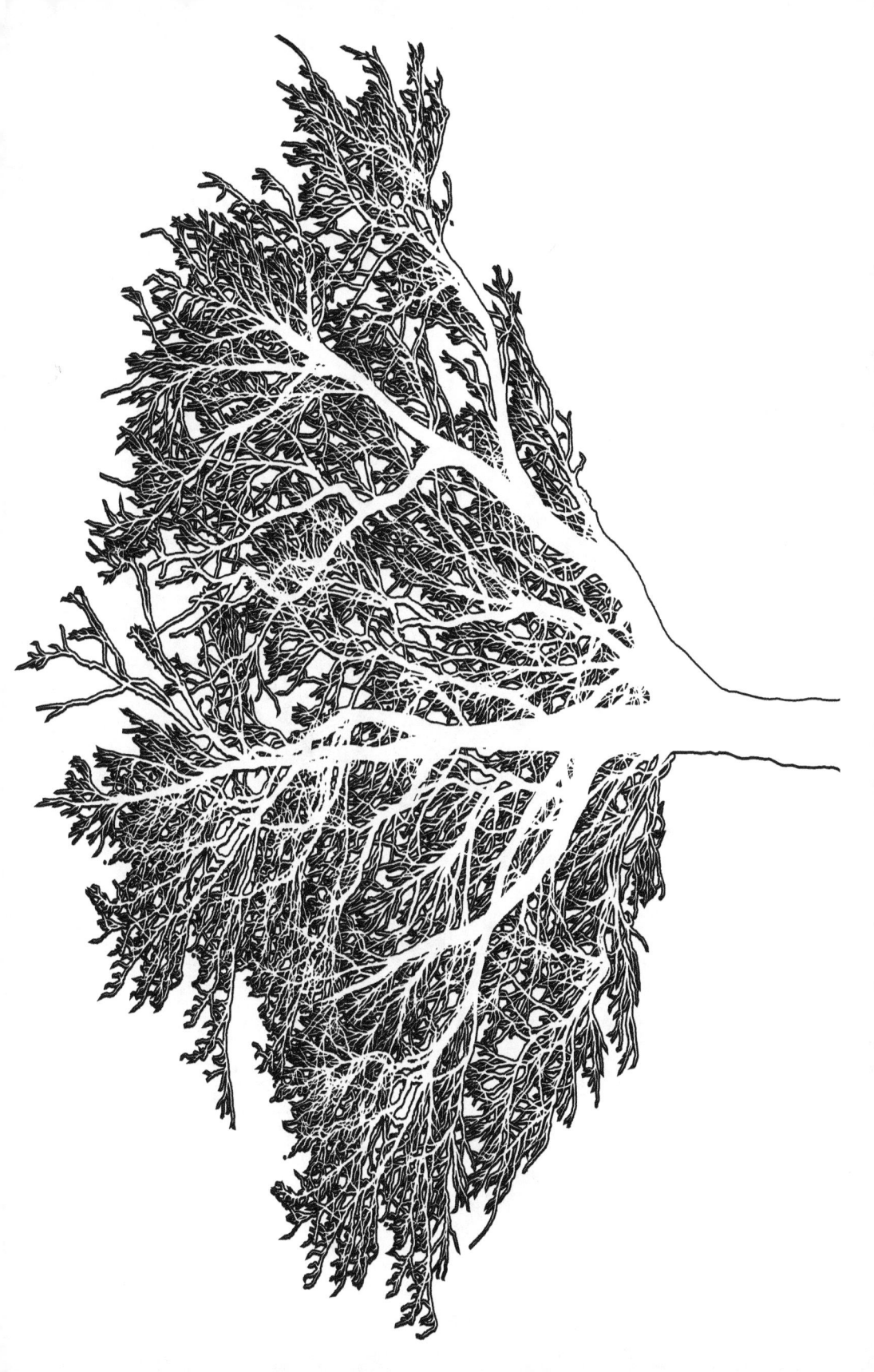

Visit
www.AdultColoringPages.net
for more coloring goodness

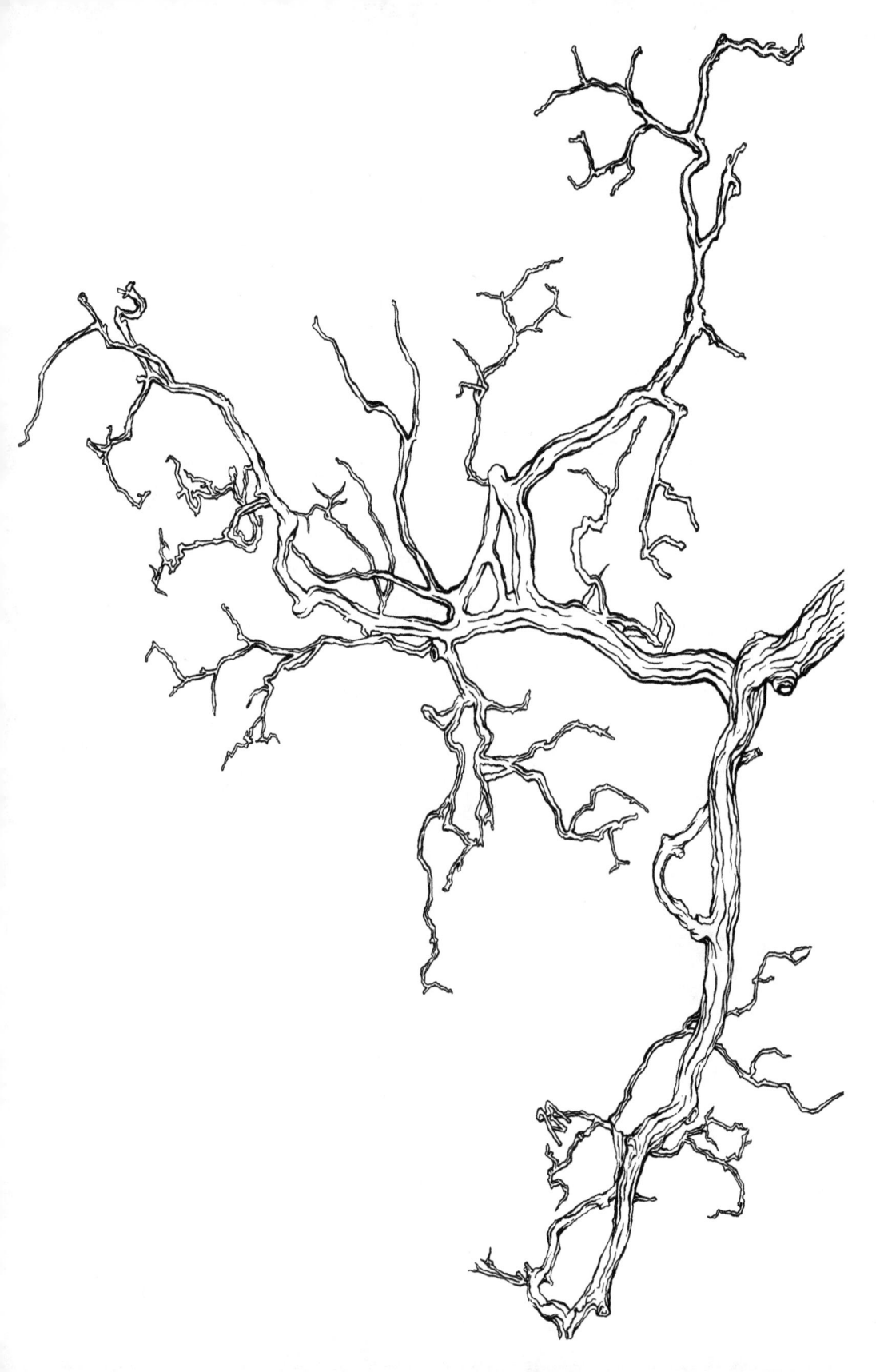

Visit

www.AdultColoringPages.net

for more coloring goodness

Visit
www.AdultColoringPages.net
for more coloring goodness

Visit

www.AdultColoringPages.net

for more coloring goodness

Visit

www.AdultColoringPages.net

for more coloring goodness

Visit

www.AdultColoringPages.net

for more coloring goodness

Visit

www.AdultColoringPages.net

for more coloring goodness

Visit

www.AdultColoringPages.net

for more coloring goodness

Visit
www.AdultColoringPages.net
for more coloring goodness

Visit
www.AdultColoringPages.net
for more coloring goodness

Visit
www.AdultColoringPages.net
for more coloring goodness

Visit

www.AdultColoringPages.net

for more coloring goodness

Visit
www.AdultColoringPages.net
for more coloring goodness

Visit

www.AdultColoringPages.net

for more coloring goodness

Visit

www.AdultColoringPages.net

for more coloring goodness

Visit

www.AdultColoringPages.net

for more coloring goodness

Visit

www.AdultColoringPages.net

for more coloring goodness

Visit
www.AdultColoringPages.net
for more coloring goodness

Visit
www.AdultColoringPages.net
for more coloring goodness

Visit
www.AdultColoringPages.net
for more coloring goodness

Visit

www.AdultColoringPages.net

for more coloring goodness

Visit
www.AdultColoringPages.net
for more coloring goodness

Visit

www.AdultColoringPages.net

for more coloring goodness

Visit

www.AdultColoringPages.net

for more coloring goodness

Visit
www.AdultColoringPages.net
for more coloring goodness

Visit
www.AdultColoringPages.net
for more coloring goodness

Visit
www.AdultColoringPages.net
for more coloring goodness

Visit

www.AdultColoringPages.net

for more coloring goodness

Visit

www.AdultColoringPages.net

for more coloring goodness

Also Available for Your Coloring Pleasure:

Mandala Coloring Pages, ISBN 978-1-939169-04-4

Geometric Coloring Pages, ISBN 978-1-939169-05-1

www.ingramcontent.com/pod-product-compliance
Lightning Source LLC
Chambersburg PA
CBHW071501070426
42452CB00041B/2072